31 Days To Reconnect With God

TOM HOGSED

31 Days To Reconnect With God
Copyright © 2018 Tom Hogsed
Print ISBN: 9781791668860

All rights reserved. No part of this publication may be reproduced, stored in a retrieval system, or transmitted in any form or by any means - electronic, mechanical, photocopy, recording, or any other - except for brief quotations in printed reviews, without prior permission of the author.

For more information about the author, visit tomhogsed.co or email tom@tomhogsed.co.

Scripture Usage
All Scripture quotations marked NKJV are taken from the New King James Version®, copyright © 1982 by Thomas Nelson. Used by permission. All rights reserved.

Scripture quotations marked NLT are taken from the Holy Bible, New Living Translation, copyright ©1996, 2004, 2015 by Tyndale House Foundation. Used by permission of Tyndale House Publishers, Inc., Carol Stream, Illinois 60188. All rights reserved.

Book Cover
Photo: Woman Looking Down Road by IOFOTO via Canva.com

DEDICATION

To anyone who has ever felt like they don't measure up, these words are for you. I have spent my life feeling as if I don't measure up…especially when I compare where I am to where I should be. It is easy to get derailed in your connection with God and then beat yourself up because you should have known better. I'm thankful for a God who is merciful, which means He often withholds what I really deserve for straying away from Him.

My prayer is that you would once again find your footing in the journey of faith.

The easy way out is to simply stop your journey or refuse to change directions.

The hard work is to surrender your path to follow God's ways no matter what the future may hold.

I write these words for the worn out, exhausted follower of Christ who may have lost his way, but wants to begin reconnecting with God. You are not alone.

TABLE OF CONTENTS

INTRODUCTION: I May Be Lost 8

INSTRUCTION: How to Read This Book 11

DAY 1: Every Journey Starts Here 14

DAY 2: Facing the Past 18

DAY 3: Mending Broken Relationships 22

DAY 4: Moving On From What Cannot Be Changed 26

DAY 5: Stop Pointing Fingers 30

DAY 6: The Flip-Side of Success 33

DAY 7: Learning To Be Content 36

DAY 8: Why Do I Feel Far From God? 39

DAY 9: Using God 42

DAY 10: Forming Good Habits 45

DAY 11: Giving God a Voice 48

DAY 12: Responding to God's Voice 51

DAY 13: Surrounding Myself With Others 54

DAY 14: Meeting God in Nature 57

DAY 15: Halfway There 60

DAY 16: Doing Necessary Things 63

DAY 17: Overcoming Temptation 66

DAY 18: Waiting On God 69

DAY 19: Being Comfortable In Trials 72

DAY 20: Protecting the Heart 75

DAY 21: There Is Someone Who Hates You 78

DAY 22: The Heart of the Matter 81

DAY 23: Spending Time With Those Who Need Jesus 84

DAY 24: Helping Those Who Are Maturing 88

DAY 25: Don't Stand Still. Get Moving. 91

DAY 26: Watch Your Reaction 94

DAY 27: From Bad To Good 97

DAY 28: Called To Be Different 100

DAY 29: Second Chance At Life 103

DAY 30: Start Again 106

DAY 31: How's Your Health 109

What Do I Do Tomorrow? 112

Have You Been Forgiven by God? 113

ACKNOWLEDGMENTS

This one is for my mom. Many times throughout my life, she told me I should write a book of devotional thoughts. I have always had the intention of doing so, but it has taken me a couple decades to get one done.

Back when publishing was a lot more costly and complicated, my mom told me she would help me pay to publish a devotional book. I never took her up on the offer, but I know she would have done whatever was necessary to make this book a reality. Now that publishing is much easier (and cheaper), I want to acknowledge my mom as one of the reasons why I write these words. She knew I enjoyed writing and wanted me to use it for good. I'm thankful for a wonderful mother who has always encouraged me along the way.

INTRODUCTION: I MAY BE LOST

It can be easy to get off the right path in life. There is not always a giant leap off the path, but it is often several small steps in the wrong direction that take us further from where we should be going. Most people do not wake up one morning and decide to abandon the proper path in life, but they simply ignore the importance of consistent, daily obedience and surrender to God's way of life.

In this moment, evaluate the path you're traveling in life. Do you like your location? Will the direction you are traveling help you arrive in the right places? If not, it's time to take a step in the right direction.

How do you guide yourself back onto the right path? Getting back on track is not an overnight occurrence, but a commitment to listening and talking to God each day.

Any time you read the Bible, you are listening to God. Any time you whisper a prayer to Him in response to His Word, you are talking to your Creator and Lord. When God's Word becomes the loudest voice in your life and you begin to follow His direction, you'll find your footing once again.

All of us slip, fall, and find ourselves in places where we do not want to be. You can either stay where you are or seek God's help and allow Him to become your Guide along life's path. Before you begin this journey of getting back on the right path, take some time to honestly evaluate your current position on the path of life.

Are you traveling in the right direction? Why or why not?

_____
_____
_____
_____
_____

Can you identify a decision or a moment in time when you began getting off track in life? If so, what decision or what moment?

_____
_____
_____
_____
_____

What two things would you change about your life?

_____
_____
_____
_____
_____

Write a simple prayer to God and tell Him you need His help in getting back on the right path.

_____
_____
_____
_____
_____
_____

INSTRUCTION: HOW TO READ THIS BOOK

Researchers have often said it takes at least 21 days to form a habit, although I've also heard it can take over two months to make something a normal routine in life. To be honest, I don't know the exact line where a person adopts a habit as a part of daily life. In this book I have chosen to develop 31 daily writings to help get a person back on track in his or her connection with God.

Thirty-one is not a magic number, but it is a start for those who may need to take a month of self-evaluation and establish the habit of reading/applying God's Word.

Over the next 31 days, follow **6 Daily Steps** in each reading –

Step 1: Receive
This is the very first step and one of the most important. If your day is like mine, it is filled with lots of noise. There are few quiet moments in a 24-hour period; however, this step is an opportunity for you to *find a quiet place* and ask God to make your heart and mind ready to receive the reading of His Word.

Our tendency is to rush into God's presence without first clearing our minds of any distractions and sin. Invite God to speak to you in any way He chooses.

Step 2: Read
Although I want you to read my own thoughts each day, my words are not as important as God's words. Do not skip this step and simply read my writings. *Do the hard work of taking out your Bible* and allowing God to speak to you through His Word. *Don't rush this step.* Take your time and wait for God to reveal truth to you.

Step 3: Review
Throughout history, God has used the feeble words of individuals to speak truth. There are many who communicate it better than me, but *I would cherish a few moments to connect you* with the words of God…in my own words. This step is an opportunity to review the Word of God and connect it with some practical application.

Step 4: Respond
I have taken the time to write out a short prayer based on the reading of the day. You can either *pray the prayer I have written out* or *pray in your own words*. For those who may struggle with verbalizing your words to God, this step may be a help to you.

Step 5: Remember
We live in a world that puts everything into short statuses on our social media feeds, so this is a short summary of the reading for each day. This thought should stay with you. Write it down. Memorize it. Share it.

Step 6: Record

This step can be life-changing because you are taking what God has said and recording your thoughts in response to it. There is something healing and even rejuvenating about getting your thoughts out of your head and putting them on paper. I would challenge you to try this step with all 31 readings. It will also give you a chance to look back over the days and see how God has been changing you.

DAY 1: EVERY JOURNEY STARTS HERE

STEP 1: RECEIVE
Pause for a few moments and pray for the Holy Spirit to clear your mind so you are ready to receive the reading of God's Word and respond in obedience.

STEP 2: READ
John 3:16-17; Romans 5; Ephesians 2:8-10

STEP 3: REVIEW
Take a couple minutes to read the following words to help you review, summarize, and apply what you have learned through your own reading of the Scripture.

All of us are sinners guilty of breaking God's law. You might be a moral person, but according to God every human being is guilty of offending a holy God (Romans 3:10; Romans 3:23). The **only** punishment for sin is death, which was prescribed by God at the very beginning of human history (Genesis 2:17; Genesis 3:3; Romans 5:12).

Many people will spend their lives trying to earn God's favor or forgiveness by attempting to make up for their sinful deeds. They will perform acts of kindness, become a church member, try to be moral, get baptized, or do any work that may get God's attention. Although doing these works is admirable, they fall short of the required punishment for sin (Isaiah 64:6).

Death, not deeds, pays for sin.

Paul plainly writes to the Romans, "…the wages of sin is death" (Romans 6:23, NKJV). If you are trying to be forgiven by God through righteous behavior or good deeds, please stop. God's wrath for sin is not satisfied by what you do, but by what has already been done on your behalf.

Two-thousand years ago God's love compelled Him to send His only Son, Jesus Christ, to earth in order to pay the penalty for sin on behalf of sinners (John 3:16). Since only death could satisfy God's wrath for sin, He sent Jesus to give His life so that the human race could be saved from death and eternal separation from God. God did not send His Son to condemn sinners, but so many might be saved from death through Him (John 3:17). Paul described Jesus' sacrifice to the church at Corinth.

> "For God made Christ, who never sinned, to be the offering for our sin, so that we could be made right with God through Christ." (2 Corinthians 5:21, NLT)

An exchange took place on the cross. Jesus took your sin upon Himself and offered you His righteousness. When does the exchange take place? A person is given the righteousness of Christ the moment he quits trusting in his own works, confesses his sin, and embraces Christ's death as sufficient payment for his sin.

> "...if you confess with your mouth the Lord Jesus and believe in your heart that God has raised Him from the dead, you will be saved. For with the heart one believes unto righteousness, and with the mouth confession is made unto salvation. For 'whoever calls on the name of the Lord shall be saved.'" (Romans 10:9-10,13, NKJV)

The disobedience of Adam (the first human being) brought sin and death into the world, but Christ's death brought righteousness to many (Romans 5:19). The story of redemption does not end with Christ's death. Three days following His death, Jesus was raised to life by the power of God. His resurrection guarantees that those who believe in Him will also live again (1 Corinthians 15:20-23).

The story of Jesus Christ is where the journey begins. Through faith in Jesus, you no longer have to spend your life attempting to earn God's forgiveness. He has freely given you grace through His Son, Jesus Christ.

STEP 4: RESPOND
Dear God, I want to be set free from sin, but I know I can't be set free on my own. I need your help. I'm reaching out to you in faith and asking You to forgive me. Through Jesus' death, I receive Your forgiveness. Through Jesus' resurrection, I embrace God's power over death and promise of eternal life. I want You to become the Lord of my life. I desire for you to begin changing me.

STEP 5: REMEMBER
Death, not deeds, pays for sin.

STEP 6: RECORD

Spend a few minutes recording your thoughts and any application from today's reading.

DAY 2: FACING THE PAST

STEP 1: RECEIVE
Pause for a few moments and pray for the Holy Spirit to clear your mind so you are ready to receive the reading of God's Word and respond in obedience.

STEP 2: READ
Psalm 32; Psalm 51; Romans 5:6-11; 1 John 1:9

STEP 3: REVIEW
Take a couple minutes to read the following words to help you review, summarize, and apply what you have learned through your own reading of the Scripture.

Letting go of the past is not easy. When reflecting on the parts of life that have already been lived, there are numerous regrets and sins that cause ongoing guilt and shame. Regrettable moments are etched into the fabric of our memories no matter how hard we try to forget them. Have you sought God's forgiveness from your past sins only to find it difficult to forgive yourself.

"How could I be so stupid?"

"Why did I let that area slip?"

"I knew better."

Not too long ago I set aside some time to pray and study God's Word but an unwelcome memory came to mind out of nowhere. At first I wondered, "Where did that come from?" I offered an honest prayer to God and claimed His forgiveness. I knew God had already forgiven me, but all the memories flooded my mind again. When regret plagues the soul, remind yourself that **the past changes for no one**. The page has been turned. Yesterday is out of reach.

Since your past cannot be changed, why have you been so consumed with it? Past sin brings consequence, but does God desire you to live in a continual state of regret for a moment that cannot be relived?

I do not think so.

Once you have turned from sin (repented) and received God's forgiveness, you must release the sin. The prophet Isaiah wrote some timely words about God pouring out His wrath on His Son, Jesus, rather than those who have sinned. Jesus took our sin upon Himself.

> "All we like sheep have gone astray; We have turned, every one, to his own way; And the Lord has laid on Him the iniquity of us all." (Isaiah 53:6, NKJV).

Before you were even born into this world, God knew you would break His commandments and stray far away from Him. God took drastic measures 2,000 years ago when He treated His own Son, Jesus, as if He had committed the sins you actually committed. The very sins that have consumed your life, have been shouldered by Jesus Christ.

He shouldered that lie.

He shouldered your perversion.

He shouldered your secret sin.

He shouldered your cheating.

He shouldered your deception.

He shouldered your failings as a parent.

He shouldered that lust.

He shouldered that bitterness.

When you look into the mirror, you may not like what you see because you know what lies underneath. God knows everything about you (including your sin), but He loved you so much that He erased your sin and restored your relationship with Him through the work of Jesus Christ on your behalf (Romans 5:6-11).

STEP 4: RESPOND
Dear God, I have so many things from my past that I wish I could change. Sometimes I am overwhelmed by the sin and shame that plagues me. In this moment, I ask you to forgive me…not based on what I have to offer You, but on what Jesus Christ did on my behalf.

STEP 5: REMEMBER

The past holds many regrets, but in Christ my past has been erased.

STEP 6: RECORD

Spend a few minutes recording your thoughts and any application from today's reading.

_____
_____
_____
_____
_____
_____
_____
_____
_____
_____
_____
_____
_____
_____
_____
_____

DAY 3: MENDING BROKEN RELATIONSHIPS

STEP 1: RECEIVE
Pause for a few moments and pray for the Holy Spirit to clear your mind so you are ready to receive the reading of God's Word and respond in obedience.

STEP 2: READ
Matthew 5:21-26; Matthew 6:14-15

STEP 3: REVIEW
Take a couple minutes to read the following words to help you review, summarize, and apply what you have learned through your own reading of the Scripture.

IF you confess, God will forgive. Does this mean the past is erased? Yes and no.

When a part of your past is a private matter, the past is erased; however, when a shameful part of your past involves another person, there must be an attempt at restoring that relationship.

Making things right with God is the first step, but making things right with others is the next step.

A person cannot properly worship God until they have attempted to reconcile with an enemy.

Maybe you believe this line of thought to be extreme, so let's examine the words of Jesus regarding this matter.

> "So if you are presenting a sacrifice at the altar in the Temple and you suddenly remember that someone has something against you, leave your sacrifice there at the altar. Go and be reconciled to that person. Then come and offer your sacrifice to God" (Matthew 5:23-24, NLT).

Jesus' teaching is very clear. Worship of God is unacceptable until an attempt to resolve a conflict with someone else has been made.

Did you leave your last job with unresolved issues?

Have you refused to speak with a family member because of a past argument?

Did a past relationship end in destruction?

If the answer to any of these questions is 'yes,' the past cannot be erased until you make an honest effort to reconcile. You can probably think of numerous reasons NOT to reconcile, but according to the words of Scripture, you have a responsibility to make it right. Unresolved conflict with another person will always be a part of your past until you have sought restoration. There is no way to sidestep this requirement.

You may be asking, "What if I go to that person and they refuse to forgive me?"

This is a relevant and honest question. When you approach another individual with the right heart attitude and they reject your attempt to make things right, the responsibility now rests with them. You cannot force someone to reconcile. The situation must then be entrusted to God so He can be free to work in their heart.

There will never be an easy time to make amends, but it is a necessary step in erasing the past. Are you ready to do this?

Make the phone call.

Write the letter.

Schedule a conversation over coffee.

It is time to take care of any unfinished business.

STEP 4: RESPOND
Dear God, Examine my heart and reveal any relationships that are not in the right place. It's so easy to simply ignore the anger and bitterness that have built up against another person. If I have unfinished business with family or friends, give me the courage to make every attempt to make it right. Please prepare the other person's heart to hear what I have to say and bring reconciliation in our relationship.

STEP 5: REMEMBER
Unforgiveness in my relationships causes my connection with God to unravel.

STEP 6: RECORD

Spend a few minutes recording your thoughts and any application from today's reading.

DAY 4: MOVING ON FROM WHAT CANNOT BE CHANGED

STEP 1: RECEIVE
Pause for a few moments and pray for the Holy Spirit to clear your mind so you are ready to receive the reading of God's Word and respond in obedience.

STEP 2: READ
Psalm 6; Psalm 13

STEP 3: REVIEW
Take a couple minutes to read the following words to help you review, summarize, and apply what you have learned through your own reading of the Scripture.

If you have confessed past sins to God and have sought reconciliation with the people from your past, then why do you have a difficult time forgiving yourself?

It's sometimes easier to receive God's forgiveness than to forgive yourself. Maybe it is because we still live with the consequences of our sin. Or, maybe it results from being disappointed in ourselves.

What makes this more confusing is that the Bible never really speaks concerning "forgiving yourself." So, a follower of Jesus doesn't really have a reference point...or do they?

Although the Bible never specifically mentions forgiving ourselves, the Bible does provide numerous examples of people who moved on with their lives after a shameful event. The past is the past. You cannot change it no matter how much you beat yourself up. If you grieve every single day for the sins of your past, it still won't change what has already been done. Remember that Jesus Christ paid the penalty for your sin so you could be released from the power and penalty of sin.

Please listen to this. It's time to move on. You cannot change the past, but you can change today and tomorrow and the next day.

Adam was responsible for bringing sin upon the whole human race (Genesis 3; Romans 5:12).

Noah brought shame on his family when he got drunk and naked in his tent (Genesis 9:18-29).

Sarah suggested that her husband, Abraham, have sex with her servant, so they could have a child to call their own (Genesis 16)...so he did.

Moses murdered an Egyptian (Exodus 2:11-15) and later in his life objected to God's plan for his life (Exodus 3-4).

Israel, God's chosen people, repeatedly turned their back on Him and worshiped other gods (too many occurrences to list here).

David, king of Israel, committed adultery and conspired to murder the woman's husband (2 Samuel 11-12).

Solomon had it all, but still wasn't satisfied (Ecclesiastes).

Jonah refused to obey God and later pouted because God allowed people to be forgiven.

All of **Jesus' disciples** abandoned Him during one of the hardest moments in His life (Matthew 26:56).

Peter, one of Jesus' closest friends, denied that he even knew Him (Matthew 26:69-75).

Saul, who later became Paul, persecuted and probably even killed Christians (Acts 8:1-3).

These real-life people in the Bible did some very shameful things, but they all had one thing in common - they had to move on. **There is NO excuse for their sin**, but they had to move forward with life. Some of their stories ended well. Some of them did not.

My advice to you is this…

Receive God's forgiveness through Jesus Christ.

Confess your daily sins to God.

Reconcile quickly with others.

Move on.

Ashamed of what you've done? It will be more shameful if you choose to waste the rest of your life wishing to change what cannot be changed.

STEP 4: RESPOND
Dear God, I find it impossible to forgive myself. I have found pleasure in continuing in my guilt and shame. I have confessed my sin to You and have attempted to make things right with those I've wronged. Give me the peace to move on with my life so I can once again find joy in my relationship with You.

STEP 5: REMEMBER
Forget what cannot be changed so you can free yourself for the future plans God has in place for you.

STEP 6: RECORD
Spend a few minutes recording your thoughts and any application from today's reading.

_____
_____
_____
_____
_____
_____
_____
_____
_____
_____
_____
_____
_____
_____

DAY 5: STOP POINTING FINGERS

STEP 1: RECEIVE
Pause for a few moments and pray for the Holy Spirit to clear your mind so you are ready to receive the reading of God's Word and respond in obedience.

STEP 2: READ
Matthew 7:1-7; Galatians 6:1-10

STEP 3: REVIEW
Take a couple minutes to read the following words to help you review, summarize, and apply what you have learned through your own reading of the Scripture.

All of us have issues. You have them. I have them. The person who seems like they have it all together has them. It is confusing when people act as if they don't have any weaknesses, shortcomings, or struggles. What's even more puzzling is when one individual judges another for a noticeable fault. Although the Bible commands Christians to judge (or hold accountable) those who teach false doctrines (1 John 4:1-3), Jesus openly condemns those who sit in judgment of others for apparent failings. Rather than pointing out someone else's imperfections, Jesus demands that "self-appointed judges" take care of their own issues first (Matthew 7:1-5). Your temptations, struggles, and sin will take a lifetime to overcome so never take an opportunity to criticize another person for their flaws.

But, what responsibility does a person have when they see someone heading down a dangerous path in life? How do you find balance between judging and confronting sin? Paul wrote some helpful advice to the church at Galatia concerning this very circumstance.

> "…if a man is overtaken in any trespass, you who are spiritual restore such a one in a spirit of gentleness, considering yourself lest you also be tempted." (Galatians 6:1, NKJV)

The key to avoid being judgmental is to realize that you are equally capable of being caught up in the same circumstance.

What is the key to helping a weak or sinning friend without appearing judgmental? Approaching an individual with an attitude of humility has a way of breaking down barriers which may lead to restoration…and helping them avoid a dangerous path is always the intended outcome.

> "And why worry about a speck in your friend's eyes when you have a log in your own? How can you think of saying to your friend, 'Let me help you get rid of that speck in your eye,' when you can't see past the log in your own eye? Hypocrite! First get rid of the log in your own eye; then you will see well enough to deal with the speck in your friend's eye." (Matthew 7:3-5, NLT)

STEP 4: RESPOND

Dear God, I have a tendency to judge others who may be traveling a destructive path. It's so easy for me to judge others rather than doing the hard work of making sure my own life is in order before approaching someone else. As you give me opportunity, help me to love others enough to humbly guide them onto the right path. Show me someone to come alongside.

STEP 5: REMEMBER

Cleanse your heart before trying to correct someone else's.

STEP 6: RECORD

Spend a few minutes recording your thoughts and any application from today's reading.

DAY 6: THE FLIP-SIDE OF SUCCESS

STEP 1: RECEIVE
Pause for a few moments and pray for the Holy Spirit to clear your mind so you are ready to receive the reading of God's Word and respond in obedience.

STEP 2: READ
1 Kings 18-19

STEP 3: REVIEW
Take a couple minutes to read the following words to help you review, summarize, and apply what you have learned through your own reading of the Scripture.

Most people want to succeed in life. Regardless of how you define it in your particular vocation, success seems to be a term thrown around in our world today – successful businessman, successful parent, successful pastor, successful marriage, successful church, or what other labels you may add. With all this talk about being successful, is there a downside?

In the Bible there is an excellent story concerning the downside of success and it's found in 1 Kings 18-19. Elijah, the prophet of God during the reign of Ahab (874-853 BC), spoke out against Israel's worship of false gods, including Baal. Compared to all who ruled before him, Ahab is the most evil king (1 Kings 16:30) and also the one who angered God more than any other king prior to his rule (16:33). He was the one responsible for dragging Israel into the worship of false gods.

As a judgment, God caused a three and a half year drought to come upon Israel. Toward the end of the drought, Elijah called for the 450 prophets of Baal to meet him on Mount Carmel where there was a showdown to determine which god was true – Baal or the God of Israel (1 Kings 18:20-40). In a miraculous display of power, Elijah called down fire from heaven and God demonstrated that He was the one and only true God. Elijah then had all 450 prophets of Baal executed for their part in leading Israel into the worship of false gods (1 Kings 18:40). After this monumental victory in Elijah's ministry, God caused it to rain again in response his prayer (1 Kings 18:41-46).

Most people would read about Elijah's triumph and think he was successful.

But turn to the next page in Elijah's story (1 Kings 19). He is being threatened by King Ahab's wife, Jezebel, who basically promises that she will have Elijah killed because he had destroyed the prophets of Baal (1 Kings 19:1-2). Forgetting about the supernatural displays of power he had just witnessed, Elijah becomes fearful of Jezebel, runs for his life (19:3), and begs God to kill him (19:4).

What happened?
Two things are clear in the conclusion to Elijah's story -
- **Success is often followed by an immediate challenge**
- **Past success does not guarantee future success**

Elijah forgot that the God who sent fire from heaven was the same God who could deliver him from his current situation. Have you forgotten that what God brought you through once, He can bring you through again?

STEP 4: RESPOND
Dear God, You have always been faithful, even when circumstances did not turn out the way I imagined. I ask you to reveal parts of me that I've failed to entrust to You. Expose areas where I have taken control of outcomes rather than trusting in Your faithfulness.

STEP 5: REMEMBER
God's past faithfulness should give us courage in present challenges.

STEP 6: RECORD
Spend a few minutes recording your thoughts and any application from today's reading.

_____
_____
_____
_____
_____
_____
_____
_____
_____
_____
_____
_____
_____
_____
_____

DAY 7: LEARNING TO BE CONTENT

STEP 1: RECEIVE
Pause for a few moments and pray for the Holy Spirit to clear your mind so you are ready to receive the reading of God's Word and respond in obedience.

STEP 2: READ
Philippians 4:10-20

STEP 3: REVIEW
Take a couple minutes to read the following words to help you review, summarize, and apply what you have learned through your own reading of the Scripture.

What do you do when aren't content with the progress of your life? The relationship isn't moving fast enough. The business is lacking customers. Your church isn't growing as fast as the one down the street. The frustrating habit hasn't been broken. An unmet desire seems unreachable. Your prayer is yet to be answered. Your day job has taken time away from your passion.

When these situations occur, you need to ask yourself a couple questions.

- **Is it worth it?** If the final result is important, stick with it...no matter what. Although your strategy may need to change from time to time, you should chase after goals that will pay off in the end.
- **Do I need help?** No one likes to ask for help, but all of us need it at certain points in life. There are plenty of people who can relate to your circumstance, so why not learn from them?
- **Should I take a break?** A day off or a change in schedule can often break up the monotony and provide your mind much needed rest. If taking a day off or getting away doesn't fit into your schedule, set aside some time for prayer or meditation.
- **Is there a better way?** If you have determined that your goal is worth it, does your approach need to be adjusted? You may have become immune to the strategy.
- **Am I being impatient?** Anything worth attaining is worth the wait. Reaching a goal often requires hard work, endurance, and patience. Overnight success is the exception, not the rule.

If you are working hard but progressing at a slower pace, maybe God is challenging you to be content right where you are.

> "...for I have learned how to be content with whatever I have. I know how to live on almost nothing or with everything. I have learned the secret of living in every situation, whether it is with a full stomach or empty, with plenty or little."
> (Philippians 4:11-12, NLT)

The writer is choosing contentment in all circumstances. When I lose my job, I am content. When the person closest to me abandons me, I am content. When my bank account is almost empty, I am content. When I am discouraged, I am content. When I am separated from something or someone I love, I am content. Circumstances should not determine contentment.

How is contentment possible when life isn't progressing at my pace? Paul reveals the secret to his contentment, "I can do all things through Christ who strengthens me" (Philippians 4:13, NKJV). The strength to be content is found in Christ.

Our focus must not be fixed on the circumstance, but on the God of the circumstance.

STEP 4: RESPOND
Dear God, I like to be in control of progression. When it slows, I sometimes lose hope and find myself frustrated. Teach me contentment…that wherever I find myself, I would rest in Your plan.

STEP 5: REMEMBER
Circumstances should not determine contentment.

STEP 6: RECORD
Spend a few minutes recording your thoughts and any application from today's reading.

_____
_____
_____
_____
_____
_____
_____
_____
_____
_____
_____
_____
_____
_____

DAY 8: WHY DO I FEEL FAR FROM GOD?

STEP 1: RECEIVE
Pause for a few moments and pray for the Holy Spirit to clear your mind so you are ready to receive the reading of God's Word and respond in obedience.

STEP 2: READ
Psalm 42

STEP 3: REVIEW
Take a couple minutes to read the following words to help you review, summarize, and apply what you have learned through your own reading of the Scripture.

Why does God sometimes feel distant? At times, why does it seem that God remains silent? Why do some seasons of life feel as if God has abandoned me? These questions have probably been asked millions of times by people across different cultures and throughout centuries. These questions may surface when an unforeseeable circumstance arises and the outcome cannot be controlled. Prayers may be offered for divine intervention but when rescue does not arrive quickly, God's nearness is doubted. The Scriptures are searched for peace, but when the answer is not clear, we are overcome with confusion and bitterness. Wise counsel may be sought for clarity, but unsatisfactory explanations may leave us filled with uncertainty. Even the Psalmist asked hard questions to God.

> "O God my rock," I cry, "Why have you forgotten me? Why must I wander around in grief, oppressed by my enemies?" Their taunts break my bones. They scoff, "Where is this God of yours?" Why am I discouraged? Why is my heart so sad? I will put my hope in God! I will praise him again — my Savior and my God!" (Psalm 42:9-11, NLT)

Is there a way that these questions can be resolved? I believe there is a clear answer.

Feelings should not determine truth.

Feelings are not an accurate reflection of reality. David wrote these words in Psalm 37.

> "The Lord directs the steps of the godly. He delights in every detail of their lives. Though they stumble, they will never fall, for the Lord holds them by the hand. Once I was young, and now I am old. Yet I have never seen the godly abandoned or their children begging for bread." (Psalm 37:23-25, NKJV)

God NEVER forsakes or abandons the righteous. Although you may *feel* alone in your circumstance, the *truth* is that God will NEVER abandon you.

STEP 4: RESPOND

Dear God, Sometimes I feel distant from You...like you aren't there. I don't want to feel this way, but I find myself trusting in the way I feel rather than in the promises You have made in Your Word. I pray that my feelings of distance would be overcome by my faith in what You have revealed about Yourself.

STEP 5: REMEMBER

God's nearness is not measured by my perception, but by His promise.

STEP 6: RECORD

Spend a few minutes recording your thoughts and any application from today's reading.

_____
_____
_____
_____
_____
_____
_____
_____
_____
_____
_____
_____
_____
_____
_____

DAY 9: USING GOD

STEP 1: RECEIVE
Pause for a few moments and pray for the Holy Spirit to clear your mind so you are ready to receive the reading of God's Word and respond in obedience.

STEP 2: READ
James 4:7-10

STEP 3: REVIEW
Take a couple minutes to read the following words to help you review, summarize, and apply what you have learned through your own reading of the Scripture.

> "Come close to God, and God will come close to you" (James 4:8, NLT).

Those words were penned by James, brother of Jesus, nearly 2,000 years ago. He was writing to a group of Jewish believers who were relatively new to their faith so James wanted them to understand how they could personally connect with God.

God welcomes those who want a relationship with Him.

Although it is amazing that the Creator of the universe awaits our drawing near, we are often consumed with our own pursuits and interests. God may be viewed as someone who is always there, but only when needed. Let's be honest. All of us are guilty of using God – ignoring Him when everything is going our way, but desperately seeking Him when life is falling apart. This type of relationship, human or divine, is unhealthy and even selfish.

How do we avoid simply using God?

The answer is wrapped up in James' advice to "…come close to God." Since God primarily interacts with us through His written Word (the Bible), reading and obeying Scripture must become a **consistent discipline** in our lives.

Prayer alone is not enough. Prayer is best practiced in response to reading the Bible. Prayer and Bible reading should not consistently be separated. Reading the Bible is *God speaking to me* and prayer is *me responding to God*. Two-way communication is what God desires. Call it old-fashioned, but reading the Bible and praying is still one of the most beneficial ways an individual draws closer to God.

STEP 4: RESPOND
Dear God, I desire to draw close to You in this moment. Sometimes I am guilty of using You only when I need something, but I want to develop a two-way communication between us. I commit to read Your Word and then respond to You in prayer. As I draw close to You, draw near to me.

STEP 5: REMEMBER
God invites me to know Him.

STEP 6: RECORD

Spend a few minutes recording your thoughts and any application from today's reading.

DAY 10: FORMING GOOD HABITS

STEP 1: RECEIVE
Pause for a few moments and pray for the Holy Spirit to clear your mind so you are ready to receive the reading of God's Word and respond in obedience.

STEP 2: READ
Proverbs 4:20-27

STEP 3: REVIEW
Take a couple minutes to read the following words to help you review, summarize, and apply what you have learned through your own reading of the Scripture.

Certain habits are disgusting, but all habits are not always negative. Exercising, self-control, good hygiene, reading, and listening are all positive habits worthy of consistent discipline. Regularly practicing these habits will add value to your life.

So what about habits for a Christian? Are there certain disciplines, if practiced, that can add value to an individual's relationship with Jesus Christ? Although there are many good habits in a person's faith, there are three habits or disciplines that deepen a person's faith in Christ and draw them nearer to His heart. These three habits are not exhaustive, but are probably the most immediate ones that someone can begin right now: Bible reading, prayer, and church attendance.

Reading your Bible, praying, and attending church do not automatically guarantee transformation of one's relationship with God; however, these habits give God the tools to work in your life. The consistent practice of these habits will help you guard your heart and keep it pointed in the right direction (Proverbs 4:23).

Reading your Bible gives God a consistent voice.

Praying enables you to respond to God's voice.

Involving yourself in a church provides consistent challenge, support, and encouragement from other Christians.

Over the next three days we will be looking at each of these three habits. Making each of these disciplines a part of your daily life will begin to mold and shape you into the person God wants you to be.

STEP 4: RESPOND
Dear God, There are some habits I want to develop in my life and I need You to help me see value in spending time with You. There are so many things competing for my time, but I know You deserve first place in every part of my life.

STEP 5: REMEMBER
Developing your relationship with God is not a single act, but a repeated one.

STEP 6: RECORD

Spend a few minutes recording your thoughts and any application from today's reading.

DAY 11: GIVING GOD A VOICE

STEP 1: RECEIVE
Pause for a few moments and pray for the Holy Spirit to clear your mind so you are ready to receive the reading of God's Word and respond in obedience.

STEP 2: READ
2 Timothy 3:14-17

STEP 3: REVIEW
Take a couple minutes to read the following words to help you review, summarize, and apply what you have learned through your own reading of the Scripture.

> "The law of the Lord is perfect, converting the soul...." (Psalm 19:7, NKJV)

These words were written by David thousands of years ago, but they have remained foundational to why reading the Bible is important. The law of the Lord (Scripture, the Bible) has the power to convert the soul. The word *converting* literally means to turn back.

You and I often find ourselves traveling the path of our own choosing, so how can we turn the other way or begin walking a different path? The answer is found in words also written by David in Psalm 119.

> "How can a young man cleanse his way? By taking heed according to Your word." (Psalm 119:9, NKJV)

> "Your word I have hidden in my heart, that I might not sin against You," (Psalm 119:11, NKJV)

> "Your word is a lamp to my feet and a light to my path." (Psalm 119:105, NKJV)

If these words are true, reading the Bible must become a consistent habit in your life. Why? Because true and lasting change does not occur apart from the hearing and heeding of the words found written in the Bible. **There is no substitute for *personal* Bible reading.** Listening to Scripture taught in church, reading a verse here and there, or participating in a Bible study is not personal Bible reading. You must set aside a consistent time to be alone with God and read the Bible.

There are a lot of voices speaking to you each day – friends, media, your own feelings – so you must fight to give God a chance to speak to you. If you are waiting for Him to speak audibly, it will never happen. God chose the written word to be the form of communication He would use to speak with His people.

One last thing. **Reading the Bible is only half of the habit. Obeying what you have read is the second part.**

> "But be doers of the word, and not hearers only.... But he who looks into the perfect law of liberty and continues in it, and is not a forgetful hearer but a doer of the work, this one will be blessed in what he does." (James 1:22-25, NKJV)

Where do you start reading? Someone who has never read through the Bible should start at the beginning. It's hard to understand the Bible when you start from the middle or end. If you have some knowledge of the Bible, you can begin anywhere. No matter how you approach Bible reading, it is always healthy to read whole books at a time.

STEP 4: RESPOND

Dear God, One of the ways You have chosen to speak to me is through Your Word. Overwhelm me with the knowledge that You are speaking directly to me. May I not only hear what You are saying, but also obey it. You know what's best for my life and I surrender myself to do Your will.

STEP 5: REMEMBER

The Word of God brings light to those traveling in the dark.

STEP 6: RECORD

Spend a few minutes recording your thoughts and any application from today's reading.

_____
_____
_____
_____
_____
_____
_____
_____
_____
_____
_____
_____
_____
_____
_____
_____
_____

DAY 12: RESPONDING TO GOD'S VOICE

STEP 1: RECEIVE
Pause for a few moments and pray for the Holy Spirit to clear your mind so you are ready to receive the reading of God's Word and respond in obedience.

STEP 2: READ
Philippians 4:6-7

STEP 3: REVIEW
Take a couple minutes to read the following words to help you review, summarize, and apply what you have learned through your own reading of the Scripture.

Habits are often thought of in a negative sense but there are certain disciplines which add value to our lives. This is especially true in the life of a Christian. Although there are several good habits for a follower of Christ to establish, we are looking at three of them. In yesterday's reading we examined the necessity of reading the Bible since it has the power to transform us.

We must fight to give God a chance to speak.

God uses the reading of His word to be that voice; however, it is necessary that the reading of the Bible be combined with an obedient response or it is rendered ineffective.

Today we will be discussing prayer, which is another good habit closely related to Bible reading. While reading the Bible can be understood as listening to the voice of God, prayer can be understood as God listening to my voice. Prayer is a moment in time when God is my audience.

Because there is no special "formula" found in Scripture concerning prayer, the words we pray must come from a **genuine** expression of praise, repentance, submission, or desperation. When you receive good in your life, you verbally acknowledge that all good things come from Him (James 1:17). If you have sinned, you verbally admit your wrongdoing to God and ask for His forgiveness (1 John 1:9). When an opportunity enters your life, you verbally submit to do what would best reflect the heart of God (Psalm 40:8). If you are overwhelmed by circumstances, you verbally confess your need for God's help (Philippians 4:6-7). God will hear these prayers.

How often or how long should you pray? There is no right answer to that question; in fact, it is probably a wrong question. Every moment should be lived in prayer. Your heart should always be communing with God – at work, at home, in recreation, in conversations with friends. Prayer should never be far from your lips.

STEP 4: RESPOND
Dear God, When You speak to me through the reading of Your Word, I want to respond to You through prayer. Instead of having a one-sided conversation, I want to make sure we are talking to each other. I want my words to be genuine, honest, and from the heart.

STEP 5: REMEMBER
Prayer is an admission that I need God in my life.

STEP 6: RECORD
Spend a few minutes recording your thoughts and any application from today's reading.

DAY 13: SURROUNDING MYSELF WITH OTHERS

STEP 1: RECEIVE
Pause for a few moments and pray for the Holy Spirit to clear your mind so you are ready to receive the reading of God's Word and respond in obedience.

STEP 2: READ
Ecclesiastes 4:9-12; Acts 2:40-47

STEP 3: REVIEW
Take a couple minutes to read the following words to help you review, summarize, and apply what you have learned through your own reading of the Scripture.

The first two habits we discussed, Bible reading and prayer, are mostly private disciplines; however, the habit we are examining today is more of a *public* habit. Being involved in a local church is a habit that is very important to the growth and stability of someone who follows Christ. According to Acts 2:40-47, the church is comprised of those who have believed in Christ and publicly expressed their faith through baptism (Acts 2:40-41).

In Acts 2 the early church came together for the following purposes: learning the Scriptures (Acts 2:42a), fellowship (Acts 2:42b), observing the Lord's Supper (Acts 2:42c), and prayer (Acts 2:42d). It is evident that the early church was supposed to consistently gather together; in fact, the early church gathered in the temple daily to worship and then went house to house to share in fellowship with each other. God did not intend for His followers to be alone in their spiritual journey. He wanted them to be together.

Even though the church did not exist in the Old Testament, the book of Ecclesiastes provides great wisdom concerning the value of being together.

> "Two are better than one, because they have a good reward for their labor. For if they fall, one will lift up his companion. But woe to him who is alone when he falls, for he has no one to help him up. Again, if two lie down together, they will keep warm; but how can one be warm alone? Though one may be overpowered by another, two can withstand him. And a threefold cord is not quickly broken." (Ecclesiastes 4:9-12, NKJV)

While one of the primary purposes for the church is offering worship to God for who He is and what He has done, God also intended those who believe in Jesus Christ to establish fellowship with each other to stay faithful and accountable in their faith.

God knew that we would need others to encourage us in remaining true to Him.

If Christians need each other, why is it that being with the church is not a priority on our calendar? Families and individuals should be able to find a couple hours a week to worship Christ corporately and use their gifts to serve Him. Since Christ gave His life for the church (Ephesians 5:25), the church is important to Him; therefore, being involved in your local church is a necessary habit to establish.

STEP 4: RESPOND
Dear God, Thank You for surrounding me with others who are willing to help me be faithful in my faith journey. Help me to prioritize church involvement and service. When I gather with the church, help it to be a place where I give love and receive love.

STEP 5: REMEMBER
Life was meant to be lived in communion with others.

STEP 6: RECORD
Spend a few minutes recording your thoughts and any application from today's reading.

_____
_____
_____
_____
_____
_____
_____
_____
_____
_____
_____
_____
_____
_____
_____
_____
_____

DAY 14: MEETING GOD IN NATURE

STEP 1: RECEIVE
Pause for a few moments and pray for the Holy Spirit to clear your mind so you are ready to receive the reading of God's Word and respond in obedience.

STEP 2: READ
Psalm 19

STEP 3: REVIEW
Take a couple minutes to read the following words to help you review, summarize, and apply what you have learned through your own reading of the Scripture.

Listening is a hard thing to do. When someone is talking, we are usually thinking of what we are going to say next. Giving someone our full attention does not come naturally to most people because they see more value in what they are saying rather than finding significance in the words of another.

On a personal level, there is one thing that seems to silence me every time – God's creation. Throughout my life there have been many times where the beauty of creation has left me speechless. The quietness of falling snow, the boisterous noise of an approaching storm, and the changing colors of leaves in the fall can leave even the most eloquent man without words.

God has a tangible way of speaking to people, though most would say that they have never heard Him speak audibly. Throughout human history, only a few have had the privilege of hearing God's voice audibly, yet we may be listening for Him in the wrong ways.

God's creation has this way of speaking without saying a word. Nature communicates His power and might in unification with His love for beauty. God created everything we see for His pleasure and since He enjoys what He sees, we should also find joy in what He has designed. Take some time out of your busy schedule to stop *doing* and start *looking* and *listening*. Look for God's fingerprint in the simple, everyday things around you and then respond by giving Him your full attention…He may be trying to speak to you.

> "The heavens proclaim the glory of God. The skies display his craftsmanship. Day after day they continue to speak; night after night they make him known. They speak without a sound or word; their voice is never heard. Yet their message has gone throughout the earth, and their words to all the world." (Psalm 19:1-4, NLT)

STEP 4: RESPOND
Dear God, I get so busy with my schedule and feel as if I'm not hearing from You. Maybe You are speaking, but I am not listening for the way You are trying to speak. Today, I want to set aside a part of my schedule to enjoy creation and hear You communicate to me through what You've created.

STEP 5: REMEMBER

Hearing from God is not only always with our ears, but also our eyes.

STEP 6: RECORD

Spend a few minutes recording your thoughts and any application from today's reading.

DAY 15: HALFWAY THERE

STEP 1: RECEIVE
Pause for a few moments and pray for the Holy Spirit to clear your mind so you are ready to receive the reading of God's Word and respond in obedience.

STEP 2: READ
Ephesians 2:10; Philippians 1:6

STEP 3: REVIEW
Take a couple minutes to read the following words to help you review, summarize, and apply what you have learned through your own reading of the Scripture.

You have just passed the halfway point in reading through this book. Congratulations on reconnecting with God through reading and applying His Word. **Our goal is establish good habits in your daily life that allow God's voice to be the loudest one.** As we approach the last half of this journey to reconnection, *allow me to challenge you to stay with this journey.* Think of this as a marathon rather than a sprint.

We live in a drive-thru society where most things can be obtained either instantaneously or expeditiously. Although all of us enjoy immediate gain, there are some dangerous characteristics which can occur by attempting to acquire quick progress. **One of the major perils in an instant society is quitting too soon. When a desired objective is not accomplished within a reasonable amount of time, the journey is abandoned or seriously frustrated.** While there are examples of instant success stories, most people who accomplish meaningful things are stories of patience and repeated faithfulness. Eugene Peterson refers to this consistency and perseverance (especially in spiritual maturity) as "a long obedience in the same direction."

Just because your friend, family member, or acquaintance on social media experiences incredible growth in a short amount of time, this is not to be your standard of success. Even though you can learn from and celebrate God's work in their life, another's personal journey must not become your obsession. Your obsession must be the mission that God has given to you and you must be faithful to accomplish it.

Results tend to be the outcome of faithfulness, hard work, and patience. Creating a stronger marriage takes work. Raising godly kids takes consistency. Building a church doesn't happen overnight. Repairing a relationship takes patience. Losing weight takes persistence. Digging yourself out of debt takes determination. Changing a negative mindset takes consistent gratitude. Maturing in your faith takes faithfulness. Getting good grades takes discipline. There are no shortcuts to the road of results.

Let me give you what I believe to be one of the keys to achieving desired results. Make daily decisions consistent with your future, desired result. Even though progress may be slow at times, results come to those who remain faithful, work tirelessly, and wait patiently.

The principle is still the same regardless of your application. When your relationship is not progressing as quickly as the next person, don't give up. When your business isn't experiencing immediate profit, don't sell out. When God doesn't seem as close as you want Him to be, don't walk away. Be faithful to your mission. Adjust when necessary, but don't give up.

STEP 4: RESPOND
Dear God, I often compare myself to other people. I'm envious, jealous, and sometimes covetous because my story doesn't seem as glamorous or speedy as someone else's. Help me to be faithful and endure even when the journey seems like it's taking too long.

STEP 5: REMEMBER
Live your story instead of trying to be a bad actor in someone else's.

STEP 6: RECORD
Spend a few minutes recording your thoughts and any application from today's reading.

DAY 16: DOING NECESSARY THINGS

STEP 1: RECEIVE
Pause for a few moments and pray for the Holy Spirit to clear your mind so you are ready to receive the reading of God's Word and respond in obedience.

STEP 2: READ
Philippians 2:12-18

STEP 3: REVIEW
Take a couple minutes to read the following words to help you review, summarize, and apply what you have learned through your own reading of the Scripture.

Necessary tasks are not always enjoyable. Changing a diaper, doing homework, exercising, taking out the trash, paying bills, shoveling snow, and *[you fill in the blank]* are not things you would normally stand in line to do. These tasks are boring, somewhat unfulfilling, and often frustrating.

Can you relate? **Stop reading right now and write down the task or tasks that have not been completed.** The unfinished tasks on your to-do list are probably still unchecked because they are not enjoyable. Since all of us are regularly faced with undesirable duties, how can you accomplish them without losing your sanity? Here are a couple things to consider making necessary tasks more enjoyable.

If possible, always do the most unenjoyable task FIRST.
Since the task will eventually need to be done, you are better off getting it out of the way first. This will hopefully remove dreadful feelings as you perform other assignments.

Think positive.
Complaining and whining only make delaying necessary tasks worse. The Apostle Paul wrote the following words, "Do everything without complaining and arguing…." (Philippians 2:14, NLT)

Ask for help.
Sometimes you need outside help to maintain a right attitude and proper focus. Simply pausing for a brief moment to pray for patience and a proper perspective can help your attitude. You are inviting God into your daily life. You may also want to enlist someone to hold you accountable for performing certain tasks with a right heart attitude.

STEP 4: RESPOND
Dear God, There are some tasks in my life that need to be done, but I have been unenthusiastic about making progress. I know that the way I handle simple, yet necessary tasks is developing habits within me. I desire to be disciplined in the responsibilities of my life.

STEP 5: REMEMBER
Don't put off until tomorrow what should be done today.
STEP 6: RECORD

Spend a few minutes recording your thoughts and any application from today's reading.

DAY 17: OVERCOMING TEMPTATION

STEP 1: RECEIVE

Pause for a few moments and pray for the Holy Spirit to clear your mind so you are ready to receive the reading of God's Word and respond in obedience.

STEP 2: READ

Genesis 39; 1 Corinthians 10:13

STEP 3: REVIEW

Take a couple minutes to read the following words to help you review, summarize, and apply what you have learned through your own reading of the Scripture.

Can you imagine going to work every day where the master's wife begged you to have an inappropriate relationship with her? As awkward as that may sound, the pages of Scripture reveal a young man named Joseph who faced this exact predicament (Genesis 39). Each day he was at work, his master's wife attempted to seduce him by saying "sleep with me" (Genesis 39:7).

Although Joseph had numerous opportunities to sleep with this woman, he modeled excellent character by continually resisting temptation.

> "Look, my master trusts me with everything in his entire household. No one here has more authority than I do. He has held back nothing from me except you, because you are his wife. How could I do such a wicked thing? It would be a great sin against God." (Genesis 37:8-9, NLT)

Joseph's response to this seductive woman is worthy of emulation in your life. If you are encountering a barrage of temptation, learn how to walk away. **Although temptation seems irresistible, God promises an escape for those who desire to be obedient to Him.** Pay close attention to Paul's words to the church at Corinth.

> "No temptation has overtaken you except such as is common to man; but God is faithful, who will not allow you to be tempted beyond what you are able, but with the temptation will also make the way of escape, that you may be able to bear it." (1 Corinthians 10:13, NKJV)

Get honest with yourself. Are you letting some areas slide? Have you allowed something or someone to come into your life that should not be there? Being tempted is not a sin, but giving into it is. Look for the escape route.

STEP 4: RESPOND

Dear God, When I examine my life, I know there are areas where I am giving into temptation. Today, I am embracing Your promise to deliver me from temptation by looking for the way out. Give me the resistance and endurance of Joseph.

STEP 5: REMEMBER

Temptation always has an exit door.

STEP 6: RECORD

Spend a few minutes recording your thoughts and any application from today's reading.

DAY 18: WAITING ON GOD

STEP 1: RECEIVE
Pause for a few moments and pray for the Holy Spirit to clear your mind so you are ready to receive the reading of God's Word and respond in obedience.

STEP 2: READ
Luke 1:5-25, 57-64

STEP 3: REVIEW
Take a couple minutes to read the following words to help you review, summarize, and apply what you have learned through your own reading of the Scripture.

The gospel of Luke gives us a very detailed account of Christ's birth, but some of the events leading up to His birth are absolutely amazing (Luke 1:5-25, 57-64). A couple named Zacharias (a priest) and Elizabeth were elderly, but felt unfulfilled in their lives because they had never been blessed with a child. It appears that they had prayed for years (Luke 1:13) that God would answer their request, but year after year God was silent and no answer was in sight.

All hope seemed to be lost for this couple whom Luke describes as "...righteous before God, walking in all the commandments and ordinances of the Lord blameless." (Luke 1:6, NKJV) The question of fairness comes into view here because why wouldn't God answer the desperate prayers of two people who were doing everything right? **Little did they know that God was already at work...just not on their timeframe.**

God sends an angel to Zacharias in order to reveal that he and Elizabeth were going to be parents, but Zacharias has a hard time believing that a man his age was going to be able to...well, you know. The angel gives Zacharias a sign that also doubles as a consequence for his disbelief and he cannot speak until his son, John the Baptist, is born. Most likely, Zacharias prayed for God to answer his prayer without being fully convinced that He would respond.

When the same angel later appears to Mary (mother of Jesus and relative of Elizabeth) he reveals to her that Elizabeth is pregnant and will soon give birth. Luke documents the angel's words to Mary.

> "Now indeed, Elizabeth your relative has also conceived a son in her old age; and this is now the sixth month for her who was called barren. For with God nothing will be impossible." (Luke 1:36-37, NKJV)

God specializes in making the impossible possible for those who are righteous and walking in His ways. Maybe you are tired of asking? Maybe you are convinced that God is not listening? But maybe tomorrow or the next day is the day God will answer and make what once seemed impossible a reality.

STEP 4: RESPOND

Dear God, In my mind I know that nothing is impossible with You, but I struggle with knowing whether I should continue holding out hope in certain situations. Search my heart and reveal any areas where I need to keep praying and believing for an answer.

STEP 5: REMEMBER

What seems impossible is possible with God.

STEP 6: RECORD

Spend a few minutes recording your thoughts and any application from today's reading.

_____
_____
_____
_____
_____
_____
_____
_____
_____
_____
_____
_____
_____
_____
_____
_____
_____

DAY 19: BEING COMFORTABLE IN TRIALS

STEP 1: RECEIVE
Pause for a few moments and pray for the Holy Spirit to clear your mind so you are ready to receive the reading of God's Word and respond in obedience.

STEP 2: READ
James 1:1-8; 2 Corinthians 1:8-10

STEP 3: REVIEW
Take a couple minutes to read the following words to help you review, summarize, and apply what you have learned through your own reading of the Scripture.

Sometimes life is hard. You and your spouse are not getting along. The kids are out of control. Bills are piling up. Your health is deteriorating. You feel that the best part of your life is behind you and that the future is bleak. A major crisis has taken over your life.

During hardship, it is easy to allow the circumstance to define or consume you until you feel as if there is no hope of escape. **But, what if comfort is found in the embrace rather than the escape of suffering?** What if the way to healing is not running away but patiently enduring trials? James writes some hard-hitting words to suffering believers.

> "Dear brothers and sisters, when troubles come your way, consider it an opportunity for great joy. For you know that when your faith is tested, your endurance has a chance to grow." (James 1:2-3, NLT)

2 Corinthians 1:8-10 should probably be read every time you experience suffering because they capture the essence of a proper perspective.

> "We think you ought to know, dear brothers and sisters, about the trouble we went through in the province of Asia. We were crushed and overwhelmed beyond our ability to endure, and we thought we would never live through it. In fact, we expected to die. But as a result, we stopped relying on ourselves and learned to rely only on God, who raises the dead. And he did rescue us from mortal danger, and he will rescue us again. We have placed our confidence in him, and he will continue to rescue us." (2 Corinthians 1:8-10, NLT)

Are you feeling crushed or overwhelmed by life's circumstances? It may be time to stop running and start relying.

STEP 4: RESPOND
Dear God, There are points in life where suffering has caused so much pain. In the middle of some of these trials, I even questioned Your

goodness. Change my perspective any time I am faced with hardship. Instead of running away from You, give me strength to run to You.

STEP 5: REMEMBER

Trials are not an opportunity to loosen my grip on God, but to cling tighter to Him.

STEP 6: RECORD

Spend a few minutes recording your thoughts and any application from today's reading.

_____
_____
_____
_____
_____
_____
_____
_____
_____
_____
_____
_____
_____
_____
_____
_____
_____

DAY 20: PROTECTING THE HEART

STEP 1: RECEIVE
Pause for a few moments and pray for the Holy Spirit to clear your mind so you are ready to receive the reading of God's Word and respond in obedience.

STEP 2: READ
Matthew 15:1-20

STEP 3: REVIEW
Take a couple minutes to read the following words to help you review, summarize, and apply what you have learned through your own reading of the Scripture.

Ants were not meant to live indoors, but for some reason they enjoy the comfy confines of our households. These tiny little insects roam the kitchen and bathroom floor as if they own the place. Although they seem oblivious to our presence, we always notice them. All of us have purposefully or accidentally put a few ants to death.

The frustrating thing is that no matter how many ants are removed from indoors, they keep coming back. They do not go away. Failing to remove ants from inside a home usually stems from failing to discover where they are entering. You could probably continue squishing ants all day long without ever completely eliminating them. Your time would be better spent finding the unguarded entryway.

Do you spend time and energy trying to correct unwanted behavior (killing ants) instead of facing the real source of your actions? The wise writer of Proverbs gives us some timely advice for guarding the part of you that really matters.

> "Above all else, guard your heart, for it affects everything you do." (Proverbs 4:23, NLT)

How does a person guard their heart? Guarding the heart is about setting boundaries in the following areas: the mind, eyes, and ears. A person must protect what they allow their mind to dwell on. A wrong thought should be battled through prayer. The eyes should be guarded against seeing things that lead the heart far from God. The ears should not listen to messages that cause the heart to long for something other than God's ways.

When a person's heart is not guarded by truth and righteousness, wrong behavior will be repeated.

Do you ever wonder why you keep looking at things you shouldn't? Why does anger continue to rise up in your attitude, actions, and reactions? Why are some of your relationships in pieces? Why do you keep running from the things God wants you to do?

Maybe it's time for you to quit "killing ants" and begin protecting the unguarded entryway.

STEP 4: RESPOND

Dear God, Help me to guard my heart by setting boundaries around what I think about, see, and hear. I want my heart to be protected from those things that would destroy me.

STEP 5: REMEMBER

We are a culture obsessed with what can be seen while we really should be guarding what cannot be seen.

STEP 6: RECORD

Spend a few minutes recording your thoughts and any application from today's reading.

_____
_____
_____
_____
_____
_____
_____
_____
_____
_____
_____
_____
_____
_____
_____
_____

DAY 21: THERE IS SOMEONE WHO HATES YOU

STEP 1: RECEIVE
Pause for a few moments and pray for the Holy Spirit to clear your mind so you are ready to receive the reading of God's Word and respond in obedience.

STEP 2: READ
1 Peter 5:6-11

STEP 3: REVIEW
Take a couple minutes to read the following words to help you review, summarize, and apply what you have learned through your own reading of the Scripture.

Do you know anyone who hates you? I am not certain about this, but I don't think there are a lot of people who hate me…although there may be a few who dislike me. Hatred is a pretty strong feeling and implies that one individual is hopeful for the demise or destruction of another. Maintaining peace in relationships is a preferable way to live life. You should never take delight in others hating you.

Even if you do not know of another human being who hates you, there is someone who has always hated you – Satan. He wants to see your life destroyed. Peter, one of Christ's followers, wrote the following words to the first century church.

> "Be sober, be vigilant; because your adversary the devil walks about like a roaring lion, seeking whom he may devour." (1 Peter 5:8, NKJV)

Satan is actively seeking your demise. He is going to use temptation, disappointments, and persecution to try to destroy you. He is going to attempt to tear down your character, your family, your insecurities, your ministry, your past, and your thoughts so that he can move in for the kill. That's how he operates. He hates you. He hates God. He hates what is good. So, how does a follower of Christ combat Satan's hatred for them? Peter answers that question.

> "Stand firm against him, and be strong in your faith. Remember that your Christian brothers and sisters all over the world are going through the same kind of suffering you are" (1 Peter 5:9, NLT).

1. Stand firm against Satan. Don't back down from the fight. God, who indwells all who believe in Christ, is greater than Satan's lies and deceit (1 John 4:4). Through God's power and strength, believers can stand firm against Satan's attacks.

2. Be strong in your faith. The best way to resist the devil is to remain obedient to the ways of God. A holy life is no match for the onslaughts of Satan.

3. You are not alone. Others, just like you, are being attacked by Satan and his oppressors. You have not been singled out, but he is doing his best to wage war against God and any who love Him.

You must be watchful and alert to the attacks of Satan. He hates you. He wants to destroy you. You don't have to sit back and take it.

Stand firm. Be strong. You are not alone.

STEP 4: RESPOND

Dear God, Satan is interested in destroying my life and I do not want to give him any space in my life. Thank you for being near to me and providing the strength to resist the attacks of Satan. Help me not to let my guard down, but to stay alert to Satan's tricks and tactics to demolish my life.

STEP 5: REMEMBER

Evil is always lurking in the background. Keep your eyes open and your guard up.

STEP 6: RECORD

Spend a few minutes recording your thoughts and any application from today's reading.

_____
_____
_____
_____
_____
_____
_____
_____
_____
_____
_____
_____
_____
_____
_____

DAY 22: THE HEART OF THE MATTER

STEP 1: RECEIVE
Pause for a few moments and pray for the Holy Spirit to clear your mind so you are ready to receive the reading of God's Word and respond in obedience.

STEP 2: READ
Psalm 51:1-17

STEP 3: REVIEW
Take a couple minutes to read the following words to help you review, summarize, and apply what you have learned through your own reading of the Scripture.

Have you ever read the Old Testament book Leviticus? To be honest, it is probably not a very popular book of the Bible with modern-day worshipers. There may be many reasons why, but the most glaring one is that most of the ceremonies and guidelines written in Leviticus are no longer practiced in our culture today. These practices were specifically designed so that the nation of Israel could comprehend what it meant to properly worship and obey God.

New Testament worshipers do not practice these sacrifices or rituals because Jesus Christ's sacrifice on the cross paid the penalty for sin (death) once for all (Hebrews 9:12; 10:8-10), making these sacrifices and offerings unnecessary. But just because the rituals written in Leviticus are no longer practiced, should we ignore the practical implications for the modern-day worshiper? Absolutely not!

One of the biggest lessons to be learned from Leviticus is the necessity of marrying the heart to actions. Sacrifices were acceptable ONLY when the attitude of the heart was right (read the story of Cain and Abel in Genesis 4). *Going through the motions of worship to "get God off your back" is a waste of time.*

A sacrifice is not a sacrifice if you don't mean it.

After King David committed adultery and conspired to murder the woman's husband (2 Samuel 11), he finally came to place of repentance and sacrifice about one year later (2 Samuel 12; Psalm 32 and 51). David was convinced that the heart and actions had to be joined together if a sacrifice was to mean anything. Here are the beautiful words David wrote in a repentant prayer to God.

> "For You do not desire sacrifice, or else I would give it; You do not delight in burnt offering. The sacrifices of God are a broken spirit, A broken and a contrite [repentant] heart— These, O God, You will not despise." (Psalm 51:16-17, NKJV)

Are you simply going through the motions or is your heart in it?

STEP 4: RESPOND

Dear God, I do not want to go through the motions of worship without having the right heart attitude. Give me an awareness of my sin and weaknesses so that I might respond in humility and obedience.

STEP 5: REMEMBER

True worship and sacrifice does not come from the hands or the feet but from the heart.

STEP 6: RECORD

Spend a few minutes recording your thoughts and any application from today's reading.

_____
_____
_____
_____
_____
_____
_____
_____
_____
_____
_____
_____
_____
_____
_____
_____
_____

DAY 23: SPENDING TIME WITH THOSE WHO NEED JESUS

STEP 1: RECEIVE
Pause for a few moments and pray for the Holy Spirit to clear your mind so you are ready to receive the reading of God's Word and respond in obedience.

STEP 2: READ
Luke 5:27-32

STEP 3: REVIEW
Take a couple minutes to read the following words to help you review, summarize, and apply what you have learned through your own reading of the Scripture.

One day Jesus encounters a man who works for the tax office and asks him to change occupations. Instead of cheating people out of their hard earned money by collecting a little extra for himself, Jesus asks this man named Levi (Matthew) to work for Him. Without hesitation

Levi closes his office, abandons everything he owns, and follows Jesus (Luke 5:27-28). This is a dramatic life change.

After his early retirement from tax collecting, Levi holds a party in his home in honor of Jesus (his new teacher). Levi invited the "who's who" of losers and local outcasts to attend alongside Jesus' disciples (Luke 5:29). The people answering the door at Levi's house obviously didn't get the memo about sticking to the guest list because somehow the stuck-up religious people crashed the party accusing Jesus and His disciples of eating and drinking with social outcasts (Luke 5:30).

The so-called religious leaders thought that if Jesus and His followers were representing God, they should be a tad more discreet about the company they kept; after all, the scribes (interpreters of the Old Testament law) and Pharisees (a group of people consumed with external rules) would never be caught dead befriending such outcasts.

When Jesus got word that the party-poopers had busted up the celebration, He immediately defended the people on the guest list.

> "Healthy people don't need a doctor – sick people do. I have come not to call those who think they are righteous, but those who know they are sinners and need to repent." (Luke 5:31 NLT)

Jesus' response to the criticisms of the self-righteous is very direct. Rather than waste His time catering to people who thought they had God all figured out, He would instead spend His days offering hope and life to those who needed it most.

A lot of religious people are more concerned about who they can stay away from rather than being concerned about who needs Jesus most.

Jesus was never partial and was always willing to extend a touch or a look of compassion toward those who were the least in society. The church has to get this right. James said it best.

> "My dear brothers and sisters, how can you claim that you have faith in our glorious Lord Jesus Christ if you favor some people more than others? For instance, suppose someone comes into your meeting dressed in fancy clothes and expensive jewelry, and another comes in who is poor and dressed in shabby clothes. If you give special attention and a good seat to the rich person, but you say to the poor one, 'You can stand over there, or else sit on the floor' – well, doesn't this discrimination show that you are guided by wrong motives? …Love your neighbor as yourself. But if you pay special attention to the rich, you are committing a sin, for you are guilty of breaking that law." (James 2:1-4; James 2:8-9, NLT)

STEP 4: RESPOND
Dear God, You have been gracious is forgiving me and making me a part of Your family. I'm certainly not perfect, but I want others to experience the life change You are giving me. Show me the people in my life who need You most.

STEP 5: REMEMBER
Jesus spent time with those who were spiritually empty rather than people who were full of themselves.

STEP 6: RECORD

Spend a few minutes recording your thoughts and any application from today's reading.

DAY 24: HELPING THOSE WHO ARE MATURING

STEP 1: RECEIVE
Pause for a few moments and pray for the Holy Spirit to clear your mind so you are ready to receive the reading of God's Word and respond in obedience.

STEP 2: READ
2 Timothy 2:1-2; Titus 2:3-5

STEP 3: REVIEW
Take a couple minutes to read the following words to help you review, summarize, and apply what you have learned through your own reading of the Scripture.

I worked bagging groceries at a local grocery store while in high school. My job was actually very enjoyable as I tend to thrive on being around people. My fellow employees were great to work with and I enjoyed brief, but good conversations with the customers.

There were only two things I hated about this job -
- Customers with unreasonable demands about packing their groceries (i.e. double paper bagged, plastic bag inside of paper)
- Customers who were too lazy to return their shopping cart to the designated area

If you fall into that last category, you know who you are. Every shopper has three options after placing their bagged items into their car: leave the shopping cart in front of your car (extreme laziness), leave the shopping cart far enough away from your car where it does not look like you did it (lazy and sneaky), or put the shopping cart in its proper place (outstanding human being!).

After bagging groceries for many years, I always return the cart to its proper place *[pats self on back]*. I know what a pain it is to gather scattered shopping carts from a parking lot. I feel the pain of the scrawny kid in a losing a game of hide-and-seek with dozens of carts. You may not be able to relate to my strong feelings about the proper disposal of shopping carts, but I believe I speak for anyone who gathers carts – put the cart back where it belongs!

Sometimes when we have been following Christ for a long period of time, we tend to forget about the hardships, learning process, and struggles of a person who is just starting out on their faith journey. You may not relate with working in a grocery store and gathering shopping carts, but you probably know what it feels like to be learning, dependent, and in need of the help of others.

As a maturing follower of Christ, you have an incredible responsibility to help those who are developing in the faith. Sure…they can "gather the carts on their own," but it will take a lot more time and effort to accomplish the goal. The Christian life is not meant to be lived alone and we need Christians who will join hands with those who are still learning and maturing in their faith. Be willing to invest your time to help others who need a hand.

Are you helping put the cart back?

STEP 4: RESPOND
Dear God, I remember the different seasons of living a life of new faith and I want to make sure I'm joining hands with those developing in their faith. If there is someone in my life who needs my help, may I set aside my agenda and spend time with them.

STEP 5: REMEMBER
You were once where someone else is now.

STEP 6: RECORD
Spend a few minutes recording your thoughts and any application from today's reading.

_____
_____
_____
_____
_____
_____
_____
_____
_____
_____
_____
_____
_____
_____
_____

DAY 25: DON'T STAND STILL. GET MOVING.

STEP 1: RECEIVE
Pause for a few moments and pray for the Holy Spirit to clear your mind so you are ready to receive the reading of God's Word and respond in obedience.

STEP 2: READ
Matthew 7:21-29

STEP 3: REVIEW
Take a couple minutes to read the following words to help you review, summarize, and apply what you have learned through your own reading of the Scripture.

A few years ago we spotted a baby bird who appeared to have either fallen from the nest or the parents had pushed it out. At first we thought its' wing was broken because there was little movement, but only loud chirping. When we moved closer to the bird, it began jumping and flapping as if it would soon be in flight. Without warning, other birds began swooping down at me from all sides. The little bird continued to exercise his wings and legs, but for some reason he never took flight.

Over the next few minutes, we observed something pretty amazing. The other birds began flying at the baby bird and pecking it on the backside. Initially I thought this was mean but then I understood what they were doing. They were attempting to motivate this helpless bird to fly. As each bird came down from the air, the baby bird would try to take flight.

The following day I walked outside only to find the remains of the bird in the exact same spot where we had left it the day before. I felt bad for the tiny, helpless bird. It was trying its hardest, but never had what it took to actually fly. Something was missing.

While spending most of my life growing up in the church, I have seen this scenario repeated over and over – professing Christians never taking flight. There is some "jumping around" and "flapping of the wings" but no long-term commitment to following Christ. Don't get me wrong. No one is perfect. **There are times when all of us jump around, flap our wings, and fall flat on our faces; however, genuine believers seek forward progress in their relationship with Jesus Christ.** By forward progress I mean that there is a consistent desire to follow God's ways.

There will be seasons of sin and even running from God, but He will finally get our attention and we'll surrender to His ways. If God's Spirit lives inside you, He is faithful to continue making us more like Him in our attitudes, actions, and desires (Philippians 1:6).

Is there forward progress in your life? If not, stop and start heading the other way. Allow God to have His way.

How can this be done? Pick up God's word once again. Spend time talking with Him in prayer. Connect at a deeper level with people at church. Get accountable with a mature, Christian friend.

Don't waste your life on the ground. Take flight.

STEP 4: RESPOND
Dear God, I have been guilty of being content in my faith. There are times when I know You have asked me to move, but I have disobeyed. I want to follow Your ways so strengthen my hands and feet to move in obedience.

STEP 5: REMEMBER
Failing to progress is never a part of God's plan.

STEP 6: RECORD
Spend a few minutes recording your thoughts and any application from today's reading.

_____
_____
_____
_____
_____
_____
_____
_____
_____
_____
_____
_____
_____
_____

DAY 26: WATCH YOUR REACTION

STEP 1: RECEIVE
Pause for a few moments and pray for the Holy Spirit to clear your mind so you are ready to receive the reading of God's Word and respond in obedience.

STEP 2: READ
Matthew 5:38-48

STEP 3: REVIEW
Take a couple minutes to read the following words to help you review, summarize, and apply what you have learned through your own reading of the Scripture.

Conflict is inevitable in everyday life, but you can choose how to respond. Many times you may feel a need for personal retaliation when your so-called "rights" have been violated. A smart remark, a dirty look, a word of gossip, or personal attacks top our list when someone crosses us the wrong way, but is that God's standard of conduct?

In one of His sermons, Jesus throws out a couple words we might overlook if we don't read carefully.

> "But I say, do not resist an evil person! If someone slaps you on the right cheek, offer the other cheek also." (Matthew 5:39, NLT)

Jesus commands His followers to turn the other way instead of seeking revenge on those who have offended you. **Retaliating is natural. Pardoning is supernatural.**

Unleashing a tirade of vengeful words on someone who has pushed you over the edge may *feel* good. You may believe angry words will cause the other person to compromise, back down, or even apologize; however, harsh words often cause further tension between two individuals.

Unkind words leave ugly scars.

Those who claim to follow Christ are accountable for the words they speak and should carefully guard their responses. Spoken words reflect what is in the heart. Rather than fighting angry words with more angry words, the writer of Proverbs challenges his readers to react with a "soft answer," which deflects anger (Proverbs 15:1). Angry words bring destruction, but well-spoken words bring peace.

STEP 4: RESPOND
Dear God, Have I responded in anger to someone? If so, forgive me and I will make it right with them. I want my responses to produce peace, rather than conflict. Although it can be difficult to turn away from a disagreement, help me to respond in humility.

STEP 5: REMEMBER
Revenge may be our human reaction, but release is our divine responsibility.

STEP 6: RECORD

Spend a few minutes recording your thoughts and any application from today's reading.

_____
_____
_____
_____
_____
_____
_____
_____
_____
_____
_____
_____
_____
_____
_____
_____
_____

DAY 27: FROM BAD TO GOOD

STEP 1: RECEIVE
Pause for a few moments and pray for the Holy Spirit to clear your mind so you are ready to receive the reading of God's Word and respond in obedience.

STEP 2: READ
Romans 8:26-30

STEP 3: REVIEW
Take a couple minutes to read the following words to help you review, summarize, and apply what you have learned through your own reading of the Scripture.

> "And we know that all things work together for good to those who love God, to those who are the called according to His purpose." (Romans 8:28, NKJV)

These are words that are often believed in the mind, but what about believing them with the heart?

When Paul wrote these words almost 2,000 years ago, he believed them with all of his heart. He knew that God was capable of taking all things – injustice, suffering, sin, disappointment – and causing good to grow.

Before claiming God's beauty in your mess, remember that God's converting of bad to good is conditional. *Only those who love Him are promised a good outcome for their pain and suffering.* Humanly speaking, it's difficult to understand how God can bring good from that which seems bad; however, He has made it very clear that He is capable of accomplishing things that man views as impossible. **Your perspective on circumstances is extremely limited, but God sees the beginning from the end.**

You see death. God sees life.

You see brokenness. God sees restoration.

You see disability. God sees a miracle.

You see the pieces. God sees how they fit together.

You may not understand and struggle to communicate your feelings to God, but keep in mind that God is praying on your behalf. Your weakness is an opportunity for the Holy Spirit to lift you up.

> "And the Holy Spirit helps us in our weakness. For example, we don't know what God wants us to pray for. But the Holy Spirit prays for us with groanings that cannot be expressed in words. And the Father who knows all hearts knows what the Spirit is saying, for the Spirit pleads for us believers in harmony with God's own will." (Romans 8:26-27, NLT)

STEP 4: RESPOND

Dear God, I am not sure how to pray in this moment. I don't have the words to say, but I am relying on You to pray on my behalf. You know the plans You have for me so I wait with expectation for the bad to be turned into good.

STEP 5: REMEMBER

God specializes in turning that which is undesirable into that which is beautiful.

STEP 6: RECORD

Spend a few minutes recording your thoughts and any application from today's reading.

_____
_____
_____
_____
_____
_____
_____
_____
_____
_____
_____
_____
_____
_____
_____
_____
_____
_____

DAY 28: CALLED TO BE DIFFERENT

STEP 1: RECEIVE
Pause for a few moments and pray for the Holy Spirit to clear your mind so you are ready to receive the reading of God's Word and respond in obedience.

STEP 2: READ
Ephesians 4:17-32

STEP 3: REVIEW
Take a couple minutes to read the following words to help you review, summarize, and apply what you have learned through your own reading of the Scripture.

A couple years ago I was mowing the yard and something jumped up at me from the grass. When I'm cutting the grass, I usually pay close attention to what is in front of me because it's important to make sure the lines are straight. So, I was surprised that I didn't see whatever was in the grass until it jumped. At first it looked like the head of a snake, but upon further examination it was just a toad. Thank goodness!

The toad blended in perfectly with its surroundings. In the wild, blending in is a good thing since they can disguise themselves from predators; however, a toad is no match for my lawn mower!

When does blending in with your surroundings become dangerous? **For the follower of Christ, blending in with the culture means that you do your best not to be noticed or adapt yourself to the values of the culture so as not to be labeled weird or different.** Blending in is dangerous when the you ignore sin and abuse the very grace given by God through His Son, Jesus Christ.

Paul writes to the church at Ephesus about the need to be different, which is the pursuit of new behavior in daily life. Ephesians 4 reveals his powerful words.

- Instead of lying, tell the truth (Ephesians 4:25)
- Be angry at the right things, but never let it continue until the next day (Ephesians 4:26)
- Don't take something that is not yours, but work hard to earn the money to pay for it (Ephesians 4:28)
- Use words to build people up instead of tear them down (Ephesians 4:29)
- Learn to obey God's truth so you do not disappoint Him (Ephesians 4:30)

Paul further instructs them to be distinct from the culture.

> "Get rid of all bitterness, rage, anger, harsh words, and slander, as well as all types of evil behavior. Instead, be kind to each other, tenderhearted, forgiving one another, just as God through Christ has forgiven you." (Ephesians 4:31-32, NLT)

You shouldn't blend in with the value system of the world. Your attitudes, actions, and reactions should identify you with Jesus.

"My old self has been crucified with Christ. It is no longer I who live, but Christ lives in me. So I live in this earthly body by trusting in the Son of God, who loved me and gave himself for me." (Galatians 2:20, NLT)

STEP 4: RESPOND
Dear God, You have given me the chance at living a new life in Christ. There are times I shy away from living out my faith because it's easier to blend in with the culture. Help me to be distinct in the way that I live.

STEP 5: REMEMBER
Being a follower of Christ costs you something…your identity.

STEP 6: RECORD
Spend a few minutes recording your thoughts and any application from today's reading.

_____
_____
_____
_____
_____
_____
_____
_____
_____
_____
_____
_____
_____
_____
_____
_____
_____

DAY 29: SECOND CHANCE AT LIFE

STEP 1: RECEIVE
Pause for a few moments and pray for the Holy Spirit to clear your mind so you are ready to receive the reading of God's Word and respond in obedience.

STEP 2: READ
Ephesians 2:1-6

STEP 3: REVIEW
Take a couple minutes to read the following words to help you review, summarize, and apply what you have learned through your own reading of the Scripture.

Not too long ago my wife made a stop at our local Salvation Army where she was able to pick me up a shirt for a couple bucks. The only problem was that one of the buttons was falling off and needed to be sewn back on. Someone had probably dropped the shirt off at Salvation Army because it had a little wear and tear. I simply used a needle and thread to secure the button back on the shirt, ran it through the washing machine, and ironed the shirt which made it look brand new. A shirt abandoned by one was given new life by another. **Just because someone or something has a scar or defect doesn't mean it is unusable.**

> "Once you were dead because of your disobedience and your many sins. You used to live in sin, just like the rest of the world, obeying the devil—the commander of the powers in the unseen world. He is the spirit at work in the hearts of those who refuse to obey God. All of us used to live that way, following the passionate desires and inclinations of our sinful nature. By our very nature we were subject to God's anger, just like everyone else." (Ephesians 2:1-3, NLT)

The above words describe who you *were* before Christ – dead, disobedient, inclined to sin, and under God's judgment. He had every right to "throw you away" but God is interested in restoring what He has created. The Apostle Paul details how God took something disposable and gave it new life.

> "But God is so rich in mercy, and he loved us so much, that even though we were dead because of our sins, he gave us life when he raised Christ from the dead. (It is only by God's grace that you have been saved!) For he raised us from the dead along with Christ and seated us with him in the heavenly realms because we are united with Christ Jesus. So God can point to us in all future ages as examples of the incredible wealth of his grace and kindness toward us, as shown in all he has done for us who are united with Christ Jesus." (Ephesians 2:4-6, NLT).

STEP 4: RESPOND
Dear God, Thank You for rescuing me from sin through Christ. You took someone who was far from You and breathed new life into them.

STEP 5: REMEMBER
Oftentimes the most beautiful things are those which have found new life through the eyes of the beholder.

STEP 6: RECORD
Spend a few minutes recording your thoughts and any application from today's reading.

___
___
___
___
___
___
___
___
___
___
___
___
___
___
___
___
___

DAY 30: START AGAIN

STEP 1: RECEIVE
Pause for a few moments and pray for the Holy Spirit to clear your mind so you are ready to receive the reading of God's Word and respond in obedience.

STEP 2: READ
Lamentations 2:1-26

STEP 3: REVIEW
Take a couple minutes to read the following words to help you review, summarize, and apply what you have learned through your own reading of the Scripture.

At the start of this book you committed to change the course of your life through reading and applying God's Word and responding to Him in prayer. You made a decision to transform your old habits and lifestyle to be in line with God's ways. This new path has most likely presented you with countless challenges. You may have envisioned this commitment to change would bring you happiness, peace, and a life without difficulty; however, it has also brought disappointment, pain, and struggle.

Life transformation is worth the effort, but the track is often filled with hurdles.

The Old Testament prophet Jeremiah offers hope through his own struggles with disappointment and unmet expectations.

> "The faithful love of the Lord never ends! His mercies never cease. Great is his faithfulness; his mercies begin afresh each morning. I say to myself, 'The Lord is my inheritance; therefore, I will hope in him!' The Lord is good to those who depend on him, to those who search for him. So it is good to wait quietly for salvation from the Lord." (Lamentations 3:22-26, NLT).

Although you may not feel as if hope is in sight, remember that each day offers a new opportunity to receive God's mercy.

The past is gone and cannot be changed.

Begin again today.

STEP 4: RESPOND
Dear God, I am constantly bombarded with circumstances that threaten to push me off track. Sometimes I feel as if the path to transformation is not worth it and I want to give up. Help me focus on each new day as an opportunity to start over. What happened yesterday cannot be changed, but today is yet to be lived.

STEP 5: REMEMBER
A new day is like a blank page waiting to be filled. Fill it with things that will be worth remembering.

STEP 6: RECORD

Spend a few minutes recording your thoughts and any application from today's reading.

_____
_____
_____
_____
_____
_____
_____
_____
_____
_____
_____
_____
_____
_____
_____
_____
_____
_____
_____

DAY 31: HOW'S YOUR HEALTH

STEP 1: RECEIVE
Pause for a few moments and pray for the Holy Spirit to clear your mind so you are ready to receive the reading of God's Word and respond in obedience.

STEP 2: READ
James 1:21-27; 1 John 2:15-17

STEP 3: REVIEW
Take a couple minutes to read the following words to help you review, summarize, and apply what you have learned through your own reading of the Scripture.

I'm not sure about you, but when I get sick I'll do anything to get better including going to the doctor or taking medications. No one wants to be sick, but most individuals will go to great lengths to be made well. If you are willing to take any measure necessary to secure physical health, shouldn't you do the same for your spiritual health?

If the heart and mind are being saturated with the ideologies and philosophies of the world, spiritual sickness will follow. In 1 John 2:15-16 the Apostle John provides the characteristics of the world: lust of the flesh (desire for evil), lust of the eyes (unquenchable passion to have more), and the pride of life (thinking highly of self). It's easy to get caught up in the world's system, sometimes without even recognizing it. Getting caught up in the world's system of beliefs keeps us spiritually unhealthy.

Are you drawn to evil? Do you always want more? Are you confident in your own abilities? If you answered "yes" to any of these questions, it is possible you are adopting the world's philosophy of living.

Over the last 31 days, I have invited you to begin a journey to help you reconnect with God through reading and responding to God. When you make the Bible a regular part of your routine, it allows you to understand truth and righteousness. Listening to God's voice keeps you spiritually healthy.

Paul writes in 2 Timothy 3:16-17 that all Scripture is beneficial in the following ways –
- Teaches you what is right (doctrine)
- Teaches you what is wrong (reproof)
- Teaches you how to get things right in life (correction)
- Teaches how to keep things right in life (instruction in righteousness)

The writer James compares the Bible to a mirror which exposes the true health of your heart (James 1:21-27). As the Bible reveals the truth about your spiritual health, you must learn to surrender your selfish desires to follow God's ways. **The two cannot co-exist.**

How's your spiritual health?

STEP 4: RESPOND

Dear God, I know that the Word of God has the potential to keep me spiritually healthy if I read and obey it. Keep me consistent in hearing from You each day so that I may stay connected to You.

STEP 5: REMEMBER

The Bible reveals who God is and who I really am.

STEP 6: RECORD

Spend a few minutes recording your thoughts and any application from today's reading.

_____
_____
_____
_____
_____
_____
_____
_____
_____
_____
_____
_____
_____
_____
_____

WHAT DO I DO TOMORROW?

I would like to personally thank you for taking the last 31 days to reconnect with God. If you are reading this, my prayer is that you have been challenged in your faith journey and are able to look back on the last month to see tangible life change.

My hope is that you have also established a habit of reading God's Word. Habits can be good things and I believe listening to God consistently is one of the best disciplines you can develop.

Along with my hope for life change and the establishment of a good habit, I am also hopeful for you to continue. Tomorrow is probably the most critical day in this journey because it will be the first day in 31 days that you may not have a plan. In my own life, having a plan for listening to God keeps me on track. If I do not have a plan, I typically get out of the habit of reading God's Word.

Since you are already in the habit, can I challenge you to have a plan? Here are some immediate ways you can continue reading God's Word.

- **Download the YouVersion app** and find a Bible reading plan to begin tomorrow. They have hundreds of plan to fit any schedule or time of life.
- **Download or purchase one of my other books** to keep you connected with God. I have written several books that take you chapter by chapter through a book of the Bible. It has been my passion to help people interact with God on a daily basis and these books give you a plan. You can visit tomhogsed.co to find all of the current titles available or visit my author page on Amazon at amazon.com/author/tomhogsed.

HAVE YOU BEEN FORGIVEN BY GOD?

Although the words in this book are important, no one can fully obey them until they have started a relationship with God and experienced His forgiveness. How does a person know if they have a relationship with God and have been forgiven by Him? I'm glad you asked.

At the beginning of human history, God created Adam and Eve (Genesis 1:26; Genesis 2:8-25) and placed them into the Garden of Eden where they enjoyed perfect companionship with Him. They were given freedom in the garden to eat of any tree except the tree of the knowledge of good and evil (Genesis 2:15-17). If they disobeyed God's commandment and ate from the tree, they would experience physical death and eternal separation from God (Genesis 2:17). After listening to the lies of Satan (a fallen angel), Eve and eventually Adam disregarded God's commandment by eating from the forbidden tree (Genesis 3:1-13) and their disobedience brought the consequence of sin, death, and eternal separation from God upon the entire human race (Romans 5:12).

Much like Adam and Eve, you have sinned by disobeying God's commandments. Even the person who thinks of himself as good and moral has broken God's law (Romans 3:10-12) by doing things such as dishonoring their parents, hating, lusting, stealing, and lying.

Before you begin weighing your good works and your bad works, remember that Adam and Eve were sentenced to death because of a single act of rebellion; therefore, if you have only sinned once, you are guilty before a holy and righteous God (James 2:10). Whether your sins are many or few, you must be punished for sin through death and eternal separation from God (Romans 6:23). Good works cannot satisfy God's prescribed punishment for sin. "For the wages of sin is death…." (Romans 6:23, NKJV).

Is there any hope of forgiveness for those who have sinned? Because Adam and Eve disobeyed, God promised that from the woman's seed (offspring) He would eventually bring into the world a Savior to defeat the works of Satan and destroy sin and death (Genesis 3:15). How would this be accomplished? This Savior would be punished on behalf of the sinner; in other words, the Savior would be put to death on a cross for sins He did not commit so that the sinner could be set free (2 Corinthians 5:21). Nearly 2,000 years ago God sent His only Son, Jesus Christ, into the world to set men free from the penalty of sin and offer eternal life to anyone who would trust in the sacrifice of His Son.

> "For God made Christ, who never sinned, to be the offering for our sin, so that we could be made right with God through Christ" (2 Corinthians 5:21, NLT).

Although Jesus was put to death for the sins of men, He did not stay in the grave. Three days following His death, Jesus was raised to life by the power of God (1 Corinthians 15:1-4) but in the same way He was resurrected from the dead, those who believe in Jesus Christ's death for sin and His resurrection, will be given eternal life (1 Corinthians 15:20-22).

According to God's divine will and plan, forgiveness of sin cannot be earned. Forgiveness is a free gift (Romans 6:23) offered to anyone who will put their faith in the death and resurrection of Jesus Christ as the payment for their sin. Maybe you feel unworthy. Maybe you feel as if your sins are too many or too extreme. The Apostle Paul makes it clear that no one is beyond forgiveness. Here are the words he writes in Romans 10:9-10,13 NKJV…

> "If you confess with your mouth the Lord Jesus and believe in your heart that God has raised Him from

> the dead, you will be saved. For with the heart one believes unto righteousness, and with the mouth confession is made unto salvation. For whoever calls on the name of the Lord shall be saved."

Anyone who calls out to God and puts their faith in the finished work of Jesus Christ through His death and resurrection will be saved from the power and penalty (death) of sin.

Many words have been used to attempt to describe the forgiveness available to you through the sacrifice of Jesus Christ; however, listen to these simple words from the gospel of John...

> "For God so loved the world that He gave His only begotten Son, that whoever believes in Him should not perish but have everlasting life. For God did not send His Son into the world to condemn the world, but that the world through Him might be saved" (John 3:16-17, NKJV).

God's love for mankind led Him to send His Son to die for the sins of men. Will you receive His love and forgiveness through trusting in Jesus' death for sin and His resurrection for the assurance of eternal life? If you've taken this first step of FAITH, please let us know by sending a message to tom@tomhogsed.co.

ABOUT THE AUTHOR

Although Tom grew up in Charlotte, North Carolina, he currently resides in Northeast Ohio. He holds a B.A. in Youth Ministry and M.A. in Biblical Exposition. He has been married to his wife for over 20 years and they have two children. His ministry journey began when he served as a high school pastor in Ohio for nearly 14 years. In 2008, Tom and a team of 30 people planted The Summit Church (North Canton, Ohio), where he now serves as Lead Pastor. He also founded 3-A-DAY, which helps people better understand the Bible by providing resources that take approximately 3 minutes a day to read.

Tom enjoys a variety of hobbies including listening to all types of music, writing, messing with electronics, and watching British TV.

Some of the highlights of his life have been his mission travels outside of the United States to places like Mexico, Argentina, Bahamas, Peru, Dominican Republic, Italy, and Ireland. Many of these trips have made a great impact on his life.

More Info About Tom Hogsed and 3-A-DAY
Website: tomhogsed.co
Twitter: @tomhogsed
Amazon Author Page: amazon.com/author/tomhogsed
Facebook: @3adaybible

BIBLIOGRAPHY

The Holy Bible: English Standard Version : The ESV Study Bible. Wheaton, Ill.: Crossway Bibles, 2008.

MacArthur, John. *The MacArthur Study Bible: New King James Version.* Nashville: Word Bibles, 1997.

Spence-Jones, H. D. M. 1836-1917., and Joseph S. 1849-1910 Exell. *The Pulpit Commentary.* New York: Funk & Wagnalls Co., 1890.

Tyndale House Publishers. *Life Application Study Bible: King James Version.* Wheaton, Ill.: Tyndale House, 1997.

Walvoord, John F., Roy B Zuck, and Dallas Theological Seminary. *The Bible Knowledge Commentary: An Exposition of the Scriptures.* New Testament ed. Wheaton, IL: Victor Books, 1985.

Wiersbe, Warren W. *The Bible Exposition Commentary.* Wheaton, IL: Victor Books, 1989.

Zodhiates, Spiros. *The Hebrew-Greek Key Study Bible: King James Version, the Old Testament, the New Testament: Zodhiates' Original and Complete System of Bible Study.* Chattanooga, TN, U.S.A.: AMG Publishers, 1984.

Made in the USA
Middletown, DE
03 January 2020